Picture This!

Picture Sorting for Alphabetics, Phonemes, and Phonics

by Shari Nielsen-Dunn

D1247305

Teaching Resource Center

P. O. Box 82777, San Diego, CA 92138-2777

1-800-833-3389

www.trcabc.com

Dedication:
To my "support system"
Mom, Dad, Kiera and Connor

To my mentors
Dr. Donald Bear and Dr. Shane Templeton

Published by
Teaching Resource Center
P.O. Box 82777
San Diego, CA 92138

Edited by Laura Woodard
Design and production by Janis Poe
Illustrations by Linda Starr

Printed in the United States of America
ISBN: 1-56785-060-x

Contents

Section III: Initial Blend and Digraph Sorts, Emergent Level/Beginning Level

Section IV: Short Vowel Sorts, Beginning Level

Section V: Short to Long Vowel and Long to Long Vowel Comparison Sorts
Late Beginning Level/Early-Middle Transitional Level

Appendix

Introduction

Picture sorting is an effective way to teach phonics and develop phonological awareness. As a primary and intermediate classroom teacher, I developed these picture sorts to help my students correctly identify the sounds in our language.

I had noticed that my students were not effectively learning to identify sounds through lists of spelling words. They weren't developing any concrete knowledge of phonics. Some were learning the concepts, but the majority of my "at-risk" students, including my English Language Learners, Special Education students, and other disadvantaged students, were not able to incorporate and utilize the concepts. The spelling book series our district was using at the time was not designed well. The students would match the wrong word to a picture on the worksheet. They were often making logical connections, but did not have the opportunity on the worksheet to justify their thinking. The spelling series took the approach that students should learn the parts of a word first, but then did not introduce the words containing those parts. I thought the students would have more success if they were able to look at both the whole word and the sound parts.

Another important piece missing from my instruction was the opportunity for students to have many repeated interactions with the letters, sounds, and concepts we were working with. The spelling book typically introduced a concept with one lesson and didn't readdress it until the review section of the chapter.

Finally, I noticed that I was spending more time explaining how to do the worksheet than I was actually teaching the concept. I continued to search for more effective techniques and materials.

Finally, I found a way to address these concerns. My school, which is located near the University of Nevada, Reno, was chosen as a demonstration campus for professors Donald Bear and Shane Templeton's developing theories on word study. Donald Bear utilized my classroom for testing beginning reading and word study practices. This experience, along with the professors' invaluable book *Words Their Way: Word Study for Phonics, Vocabulary, and Spelling Instruction,* written in collaboration with Marcia Invernizzi and Francine Johnston, exposed me to a whole new way of teaching that involved active exploration and examination of word features that are within a child's stage of literacy development as assessed by the teacher. The book provided me with the rationales, goals, and lists of materials for implementing picture sorting in my classroom. So, I began.

Trying it on...

Picture sorting dramatically changed my teaching. I came to understand that there's a continuum of learning in language skills and that effectively identifying my students' place on that continuum was the first step. Once we started picture sorting, my students moved further and faster through the stages of literacy development than they could have without it. This game-like, interactive phonics activity made sense not only to me but to *them*.

Sorting pictures gave the students a stronger oral language base than looking at the sounds in isolation on a worksheet. They were now dealing with words at a visual level, so they could analyze the speech sounds that went with the pictures. Therefore, they had a phonological underpinning they hadn't had when just looking at written words and letter combinations. They were able to approach phonics at a more concrete level of learning, which they were missing because of their confusion.

Students began employing higher-level critical thinking skills to make their decisions while sorting; for once, they were determining the similarities and differences among the pictures and features. In addition, I now had the ability to provide multiple examples that the students could study. They were able to move from the known to the unknown by first removing any pictures they were unsure of and then bringing them in later. I was able to use careful observation to decide whether to reuse a sort or move on to another sort. The best part for me was not having to spend time repeating instructions on how to do a new workbook page. The procedure was always the same, no matter what pictures I was having them sort. Once the students knew the procedure, they were able to direct themselves. Success!

As a literacy coordinator, I have the opportunity to work with students at many levels. I wondered if picture sorting would work with older students. I tried it. First, I found that older students could use the pictures to help them learn, or relearn, the difference between short and long vowel sounds. Having learned to hear and feel the difference in these sounds, they began to pay attention to the differences in their writing of words like *plan* and *plain*, and *hoping* and *hopping*. They were able to move on to word sorts in order to look at distinctions such as one- and two-syllable words.

Are these pictures and sorts appropriate for older students? Yes. Beginning readers are all ages; Second Language Learners enter our classes at all stages of English language acquisition. They are among the many students who need to work on learning the relationships between the letters and sounds.

Now that we know that picture sorting works, where do we begin? Let's start with the children. Let's take a look at what they're doing and at what levels. That will tell us where to begin in phonics instruction and developing phonological awareness.

What do they know?

Educational research categorizes children's learning into stages to help with planning instruction. Picture sorting is particularly appropriate for students in the Emergent, Beginning, and Early Transitional stages of reading. To help identify where students are, there are many informal assessments available. *Developing Literacy: An Integrated Approach to Assessment and Instruction* (Bear & Barone, 1998) explains several valuable assessments that can be administered in whole-class and small-group settings as well as with individual students to help determine where to begin instruction. Below is a brief overview of the stages.

Children who are **Emergent Readers/Emergent Spellers** may scribble letters and numbers, pretend to read or write, and memorize simple books with high picture support. They are usually able to memorize simple songs and poems. At this stage, some students can recognize some letter sounds, though not necessarily in relation to any word knowledge.

Children who are **Beginning Readers/Letter Name Spellers** often can represent their beginning and ending sounds in their writing and may add incorrect vowels to words. They may read word-by-word in books at their developmental level and may finger-point as they read out loud.

Children who are **Transitional Readers/Within Word Pattern Spellers** may spell most single-syllable short vowel words correctly. They attempt to use silent long vowel markers (t-r-a-n-e for *train*), and are able to read silently with more fluency and expression. (Bear et al., 2000).

Careful observation of student work is important to good teaching. In my early years of teaching, I always looked at what the kids were missing in their reading, writing, and spelling to determine what to teach. Now I look at what the students *know* to determine their individual levels, what they are "using but confusing" to find their instructional levels (Invernizzi, 1992), and what is absent to determine their frustration levels. I'll further discuss the developmental levels in each of the five sections in this book.

Based on careful observation and the information I get from informal assessments, I decide where to begin instruction with a group of children in my classroom. Then I begin picture sorting.

How do they know what to do?

The basic goal of all picture and word sorting tasks is to compare and contrast word elements, separating or categorizing the examples that go together from those that don't (Bear et al., 2000). Begin by modeling a picture sort to a small group of students who share a similar word study need. The children say the names of the pictures and place them into groups under your direction. After doing this with your guidance a few times, students have learned the routines and procedures of picture sorting, and can then independently sort similar sets of pictures into similar categories.

What are the steps?

You'll probably want to group students by their developmental levels. Choose a sort from the blacklines that meets the needs of your small group. Make a copy for each student in the group and have them cut out the key cards and the pictures they're going to sort. They don't need to cut them out carefully; that can be done later at their seats.

Once the pictures are cut, the students can look through the cards to make sure they know them all. You can have each student say aloud the pictures in one packet of cards or have each student look at the cards alone at their own pace.

Have the students set aside any of the picture cards they have trouble identifying. This way, the students will only be sorting pictures they know. Tell them that they'll add the pictures that were set aside at a later time. In case you have any confusion in identifying the pictures, the pictures are listed in the appendix on page 200.

You can then choose to do an open sort or a closed sort. In an open sort, the students examine the cards and decide on the categories themselves. In a closed sort, the categories have already been determined, and the students organize the cards under the "key cards," or example cards. The students then check their sorts for errors. Have them compare each card to the key card as they're checking. If the key cards are *pig* and *bus* and the sort card is *cup*, the process might sound like this: "Cup, pig….Cup, bus. I think it goes under *bus*." All of this sorting is done out loud. Carefully observe and listen for sticking points with individual students.

Next, each student can share a column of their sort with the group for discussion. Children internalize, or learn, concepts by participating in social interactions in which the tool of language is used to construct meaning with the help of a teacher or peer (Vygotsky, 1978). It is during this time that students need to justify their thinking. For example, a student might have sorted the picture *monster* under the key card *hat*. Another student may challenge this sort, saying that *monster* doesn't sound like *hat* in the beginning of the word. The child who did the sort might be able to justify it, saying, "I didn't call it a monster, I called it Harry, like on *Sesame Street*. *Harry* sounds like *hat*." If a student uses logical thinking and can justify the sort, then his or her sort is considered a good sort. Try to stay away from calling sorts "right" or "wrong."

Once a few students have shared, it is time for another sort. Try to have the students sort their pictures at least two different ways. This helps open them up to looking at different features and lays the foundation for word sorting in the later stages.

Now the students can look at the picture cards that were set aside, if there are any left. In a small group setting, often students who put cards aside will add them back in their sort as they hear the pictures identified by students who are sharing. If they haven't included all the cards in their sorts, the teacher can now identify or clarify what the pictures are. The group can work on introducing new vocabulary by discussing the pictures.

The students can take the same pictures to their seats to recreate the sort that was done in the small group setting. They can then glue the sorts onto three-hole-punched paper and add them to their word study notebooks for future reference. The students can also take these notebooks home and teach their parents how to do picture sorts for various features. This independent work can be a great assessment tool. With your careful observation and the students' independent practice in sorting, you can determine if they are able to reproduce independently what they did in a group and whether the group should repeat, revise, or review the sort before moving on.

For more information on the stages and practical applications for these sorting suggestions, see *Words Their Way*. If you'd like to see students doing all kinds of sorts, there is a *Words Their Way* video available as well.

I recommend that you begin with Section #1: Concept Sorts. This is a good starting point for demonstrating the process for all the sorts. No matter what your students' developmental levels, it's important to start with something easy so you can teach the routines and procedures. Then move on to the section that matches the level of your students.

Section I

Concept Sorts
Emergent Level/All Levels

Concept Sorts are appropriate for all ages and stages of word knowledge and can be used in all content areas. Sorting pictures by concepts or meanings is one of the best ways to link vocabulary instruction to what your students already know (Bear et al., 2000). Concept sorts are also a great way to introduce the procedures that are the foundation of picture and word sorting.

Note: Students do not need to do every sort in this section. Once they get the hang of concept sorting, you can move on to other sections, depending on the level of your students. They can create concept sorts out of any picture sort.

You may want to begin by using concrete manipulatives for teaching sorting procedures. Buttons or keys work great, but many of the manipulatives traditionally used in math instruction work too. Have students count out about twenty of the objects. Follow the steps for picture sorting laid out the introduction. Allow the students to explore and practice sorting before introducing the more abstract pictures.

Concept sorts can be either open or closed sorts. Open sorts are great for assessing what the students already know about the concept you're teaching. Use closed concept sorts to meet the needs of your district or state content standards. Remember to have students justify their reasoning, knowing that a sort that has a logical justification is a good sort.

For example, in sort #3, *alive/not alive*, there is a *skeleton* picture. Students may sort it into the *alive* column, saying, "It comes from something alive" or "it is inside a live person." These are logical justifications and should be considered the basis for a good sort.

In each of the sorts in this section, I tried to anticipate how students might sort the pictures in an open sort. Therefore, the key cards have been left blank to be filled in by you or the students. The possibilities for sorts are listed at the bottom of each page. You may want to cover these with stickies or cover-up tape when making copies for your group. You may also want to fill in the key cards before making copies if you want the students to do a closed sort.

#1 emergent

possible sorts children may create: (two wheels, four wheels, misc.) (things to ride on, things to ride in, misc.) (things I own, things I don't own)

possible sorts children may create: (four legs, two legs, no legs) (live on land, live in water) (with fur, without fur) (can fly, cannot fly, etc.)

possible sorts children may create: (alive, not alive) (can move, cannot move) (alive now, used to be alive, not alive, etc.)

possible sorts children may create: (everyday clothes, winter clothes) (clothes I have, clothes I don't have) (clothes I wear, clothes I don't wear)

possible sorts children may create: (mammal, reptile) (has fur, does not have fur) (would be kept as a pet, wouldn't be kept as a pet) (lays eggs, live babies)

possible sorts children may create: (mammal, bird) (can fly, cannot fly) (has feathers, doesn't have feathers) (animals on a farm, animals not on a farm)

possible sorts children may create: (fruit, vegetable) (things I'd eat, things I wouldn't eat)
(things that grow on trees, things that don't grow on trees)

     15

possible sorts children may create: (insect, not insect) (can fly, cannot fly) (In my backyard, not in my backyard)

possible sorts children may create: (things that live in water, things that live on land, things that live in both water and land) (with scales, with fur/hair) (reptiles, not reptiles)

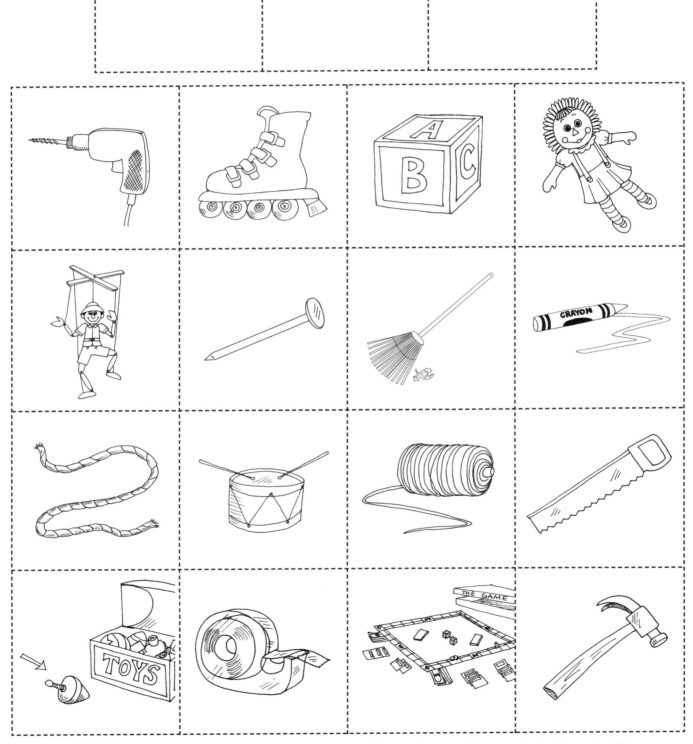

possible sorts children may create: (tools, toys) (things I have, things adults have) (things I use, things I don't use) (things in my house, things in my garage)

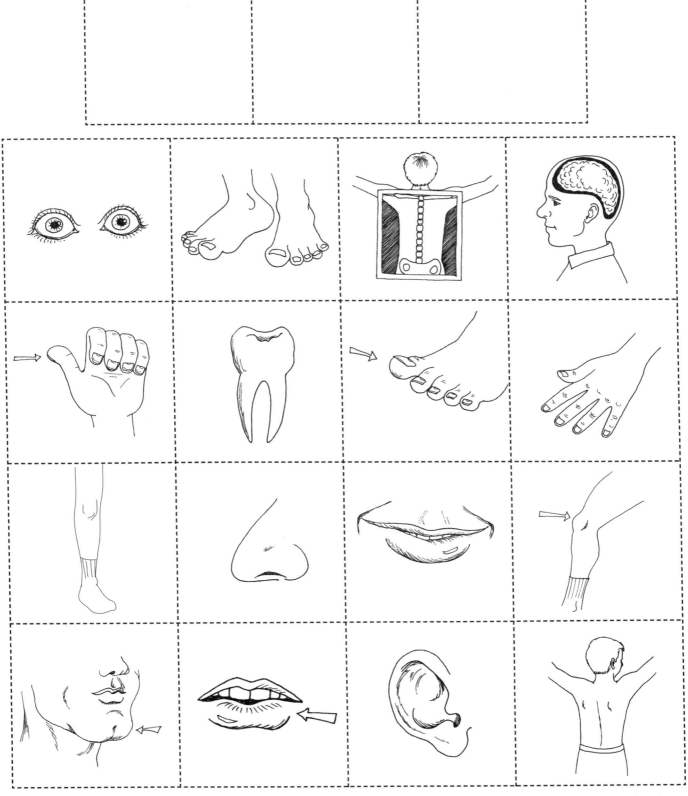

possible sorts children may create: (on my head, not on my head) (things outside my body, things inside my body) (things with skin, things without skin)

Section II

Initial Consonant Sorts
Emergent Level/Beginning Level

Initial consonant sorts can help emergent and beginning readers improve their phonological skills. During this time, students should focus their attention on the beginning sounds and phonemes, in addition to having many experiences with other reading, writing, and spelling activities. They can explore and expand their oral language skills while learning about letter-sound correspondences. Phonological awareness does not have to precede or follow alphabet knowledge or other components of emergent literacy instruction (Bear et al., 2000). Picture sorting by beginning sounds moves children along in obtaining knowledge of letter-sound correspondences.

I've organized this section in the sequence of study that is suggested in *Words Their Way* (Bear et al., 2000). Begin with an obvious contrast first. You may choose to begin with other letter combinations as needed, based on careful observation of what your students already know. Use the steps listed in the introduction (page 6) to begin.

If you're introducing an initial consonant sort for the first time, begin with a closed sort. Discuss both the sound and the letter name, and then model sorting the pictures as you place them in the appropriate columns. Emphasize the sound or letter you're working with.

A discussion of sort #11, with the key cards *fish* and *gas*, might sound like this: "Let's see which column the picture *fan* goes under. *Fffan, fffish. Fffan, gggas.* What do you think, students? Yes, *fan* starts with the *f* sound just like *fish* does. *Fan* has an *f* in the beginning of the word." Remember to demonstrate how to compare the pictures they're sorting to the key card for clarification of placement. Students will start to recognize the feature you're focusing on.

In addition, remember that a justified sort is a good sort. In sort #11, there is a picture of a fish with an arrow pointing to the gills. A student may choose to sort this under the *fish* key card. Remember to let them justify the sort. If they're calling the picture *gill*, then they've placed it correctly. If they're calling it *fish*, then a discussion would need to take place, emphasizing the sounds at the beginning of each word.

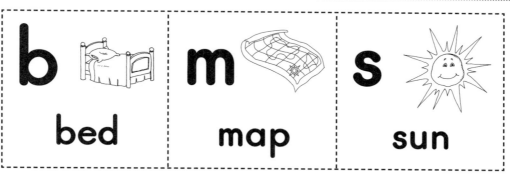

b bed   m map   s sun

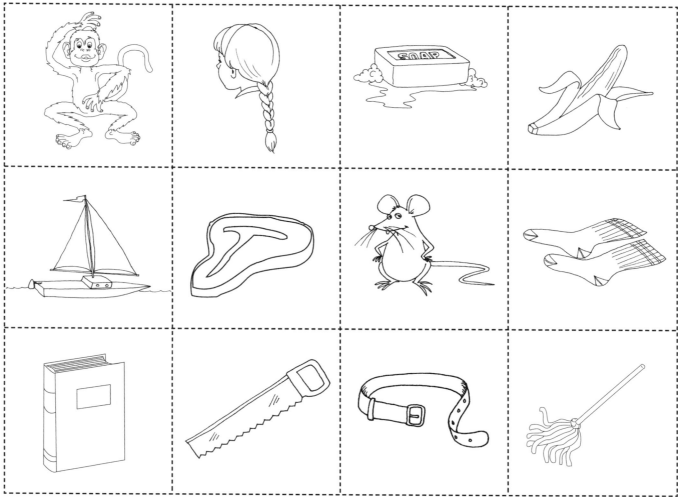

b | bed   r | rug

       ©2002 Teaching Resource Center

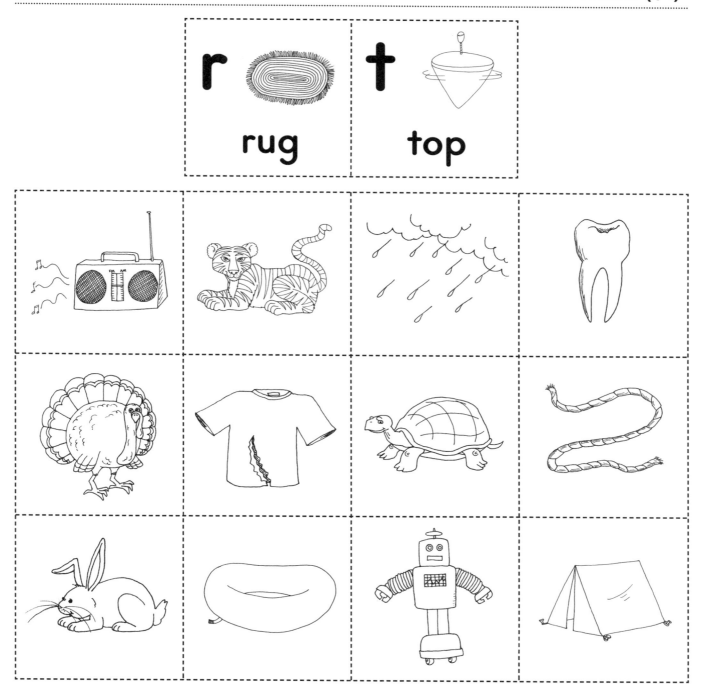

b — bed
r — rug
t — top

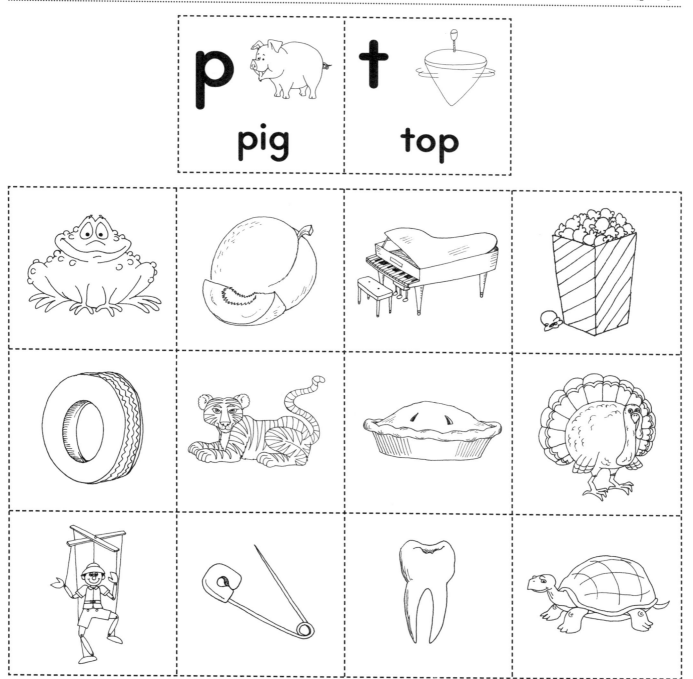

p   **pig**

t   **top**

n nut p pig t top

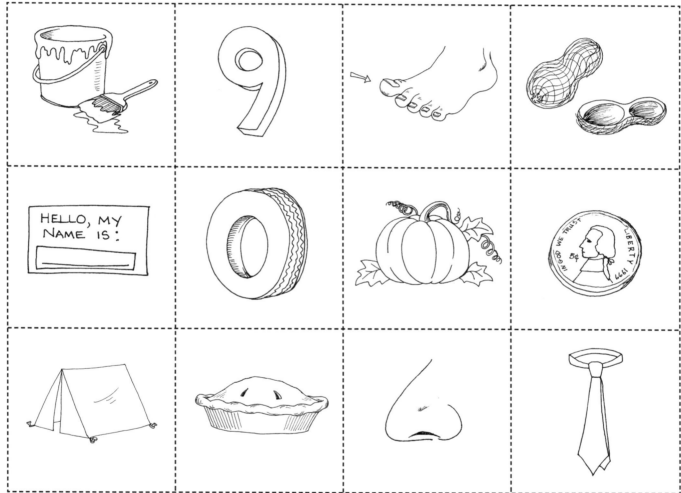

f fish

g gas

n nut

d 🐕 dog

f 🐟 fish

d dog   f fish   h hat

c — can

l — leg

l leg

w web

kick

web

k　kick

l　leg

w　web

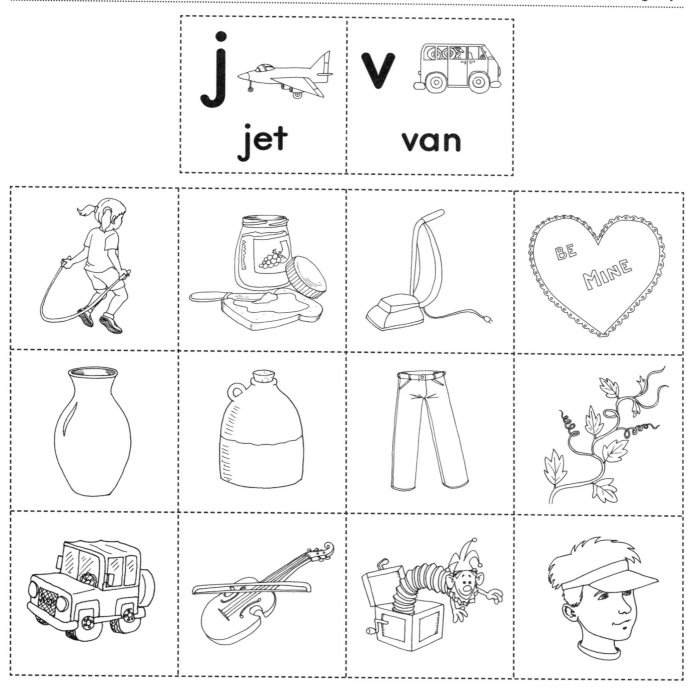

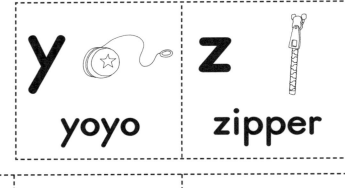

v van

y yoyo

z zebra

Sections III

Initial Blend and Digraph Sorts
Emergent Level/Beginning Level

Initial blend/digraph sorts can help emergent and beginning readers improve their phonological skills. During this time, students should focus their attention on the beginning sounds and phonemes, in addition to having many experiences with other reading, writing, and spelling activities. They can explore and expand their oral language skills while learning about letter-sound correspondences. Phonological awareness does not have to precede or follow alphabet knowledge or other components of emergent literacy instruction (Bear et al., 2000). Picture sorting by beginning sounds moves children along in obtaining knowledge of letter-sound correspondences.

I've organized this section in the sequence of study that is suggested in *Words Their Way* (Bear et al., 2000). Begin with an obvious contrast first. You may choose to begin with other letter combinations as needed, based on careful observation of what your students already know. Use the steps listed in the introduction (page 6) to begin.

If you're introducing an initial blend/digraph sort for the first time, begin with a closed sort. Discuss both the blended sound and the letter names, and then model sorting the pictures as you place them in the appropriate columns. Emphasize the sounds you're working with.

A discussion of sort #58, with the key cards *fish* and *flag*, might sound like this: "Let's see which column the picture *flute* goes under. *Fffllute, fffish. Fffllute, fffllag.* What do you think, students? Yes, *flute* starts with the *fl* sound just like *fiag* does. *Flute* has the *fl* in the beginning of the word." Remember to demonstrate how to compare the pictures they're sorting to the key card for clarification of placement. Students will start to recognize the feature you're focusing on.

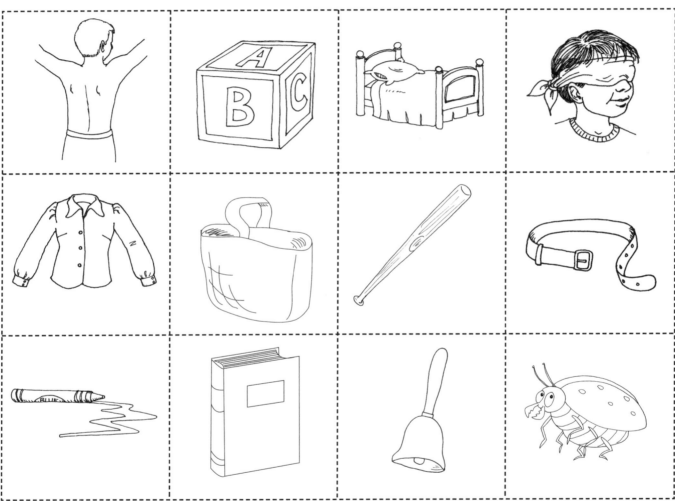

b bug   br bread

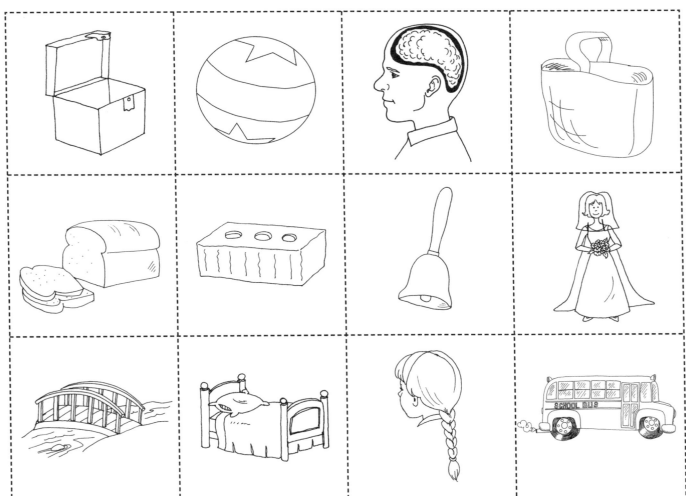

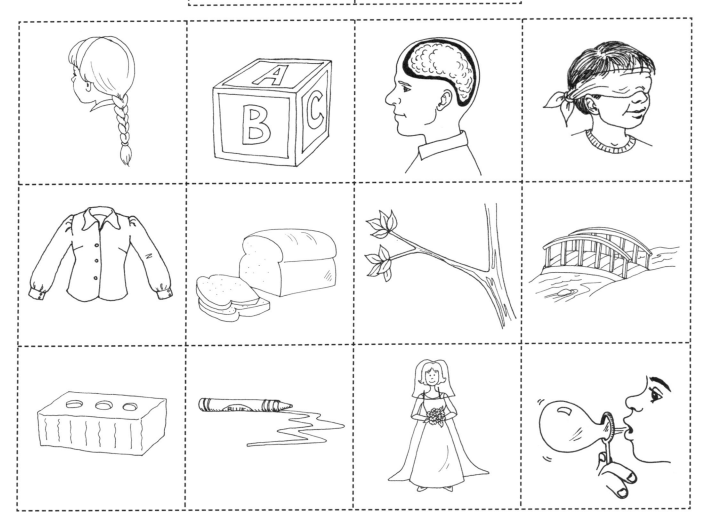

s sun

sk skate

c can

cl cloud

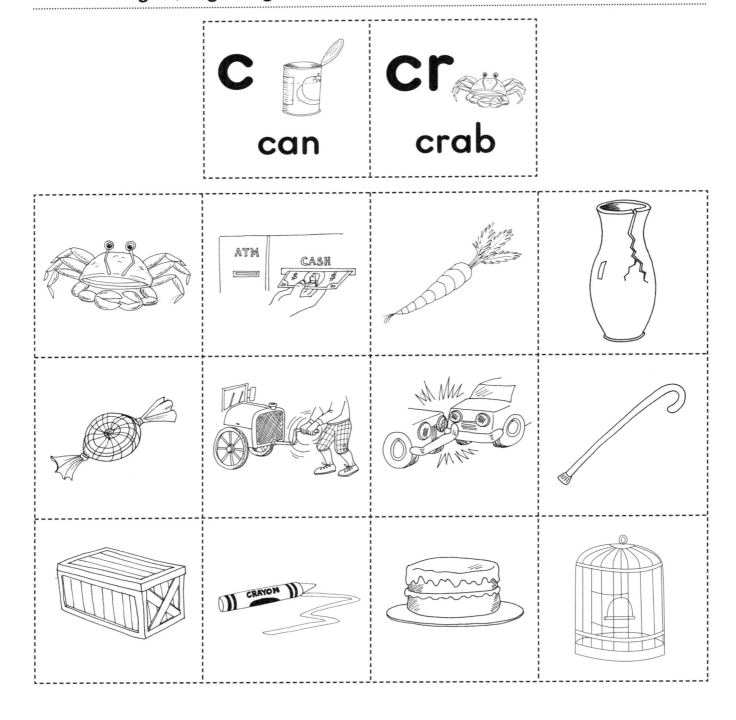

c can

ch chick

t — top
th — thumb

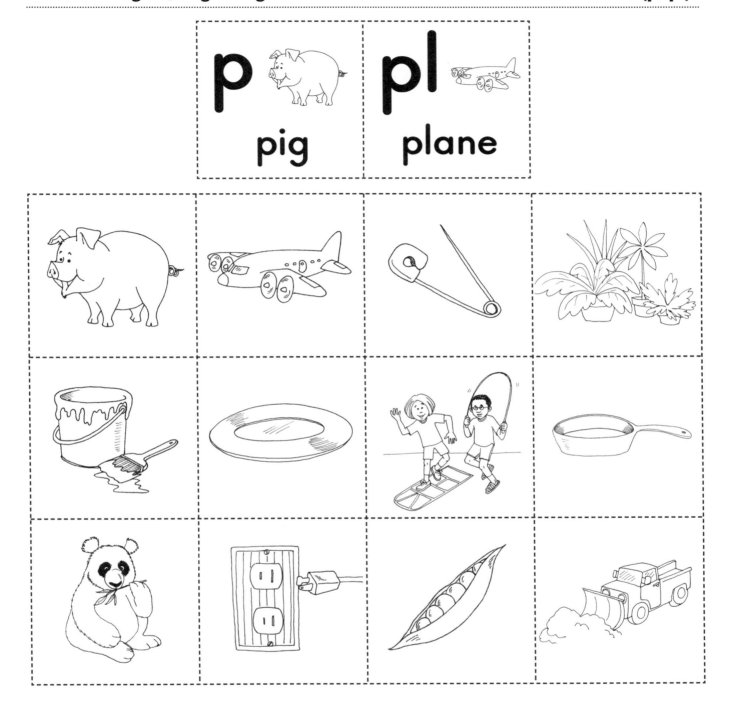

p pig　　**pr** present

g gas

gl globe

g gas

gr grapes

Section IV

Short Vowel Sorts
Beginning Level

Vowels are the musical notes of language. Without the music of the vowels, the consonants are just noise. Your students are ready to begin studying the vowel sounds when they can write words with vowels in them from memory. At this point they may not always write the correct vowels, but they are beginning to hear them. For instance, a student may spell the word *bet* as *bat*. This student is showing not only a readiness to begin studying short vowel sounds, but also the ability to use his or her knowledge of letter names and the feel of the vowels as they are produced to write words (Bear et al., 2000). Students at this level typically do not have a huge amount of words they can read by sight. This is why picture sorting is so valuable. You can still introduce the sounds of the vowels and the corresponding letters without using words that are too difficult for the students to read quickly.

I've organized this section in a sequence of study that has worked well in my own classroom. Begin sorting sounds with an obvious contrast first. You may choose to begin with vowel combinations not represented here, as indicated by the assessments and observations in your classroom. Use the steps for sorting listed in the introduction to begin.

If you're introducing a letter sound for the first time, you'll probably want to begin with a closed sound sort. Discuss the sound of the feature, the way it feels as they say it, and the name of the letter it corresponds to.

A discussion of Sort #73, *short vowel (inside* a, o *sounds)*, with key cards *cat* and *dog*, might sound like this: "Let's see which category the picture *mop* might go under. M-o-p, c-a-t. M-o-p, d-o-g. What do you think? Yes, *mop* has the short o sound in the middle of the word just like *dog* does." Remember to demonstrate how to compare the pictures they're sorting to the key cards for clarification of placement. Also remember to emphasize the feature with which you're working.

In addition, remember that a justified sort is a good sort. In sort #1, a student may call the bath picture a *tub* and may want to create an *odds & ends* column, as *tub* doesn't fit under either of the key cards, *cat* and *dog*. The student has used logical thinking to create what is considered a good sort. Allow the student to have an *odds & ends* column as long as it is the shortest column. If it is longer than the other columns, the student may need help understanding some of the pictures.

Once the students are consistently sorting an obvious contrast effectively, you will want to add words to the sort. Focus on one vowel sound at a time. If you've already done picture sorting with the short *a* sound as your focus, then begin adding short *a* word family words that the children can identify with ease. Eventually, after sorting with many word families, students make connections across word families (comparing the word *cat* to *map* and so on) and learn that the short *a* is the same in all these words.

o 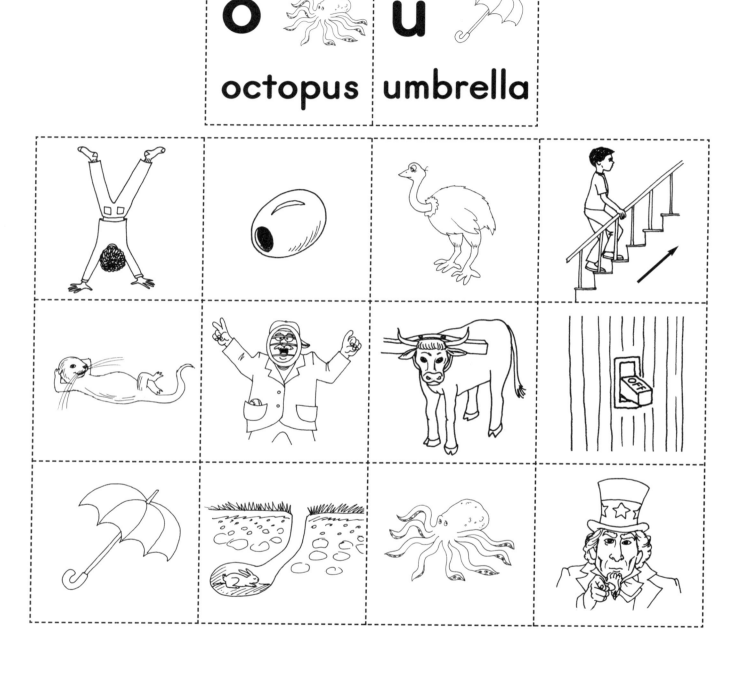 u

octopus umbrella

e   egg   o   octopus

i ⌂ igloo

o 🐙 octopus

egg umbrella

i igloo   **u** umbrella

e egg   u umbrella

continued on next page

short vowels (inside a, o sounds)

a
cat

o
dog

ODDS
&
ENDS

continued on next page

continued on next page

short vowels (inside a, i sounds)

a  cat   i fish   ODDS & ENDS

continued on next page

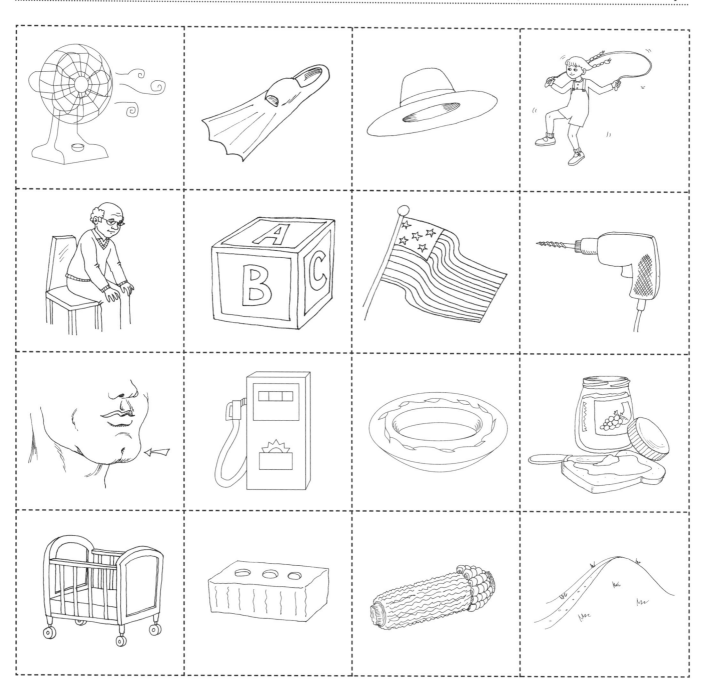

continued on next page

continued from previous page   **short vowels (inside a, u sounds)**

a   cat

u   bus

ODDS & ENDS

continued on next page

continued on next page

continued on next page

continued from previous page

short vowels (inside i, a sounds)

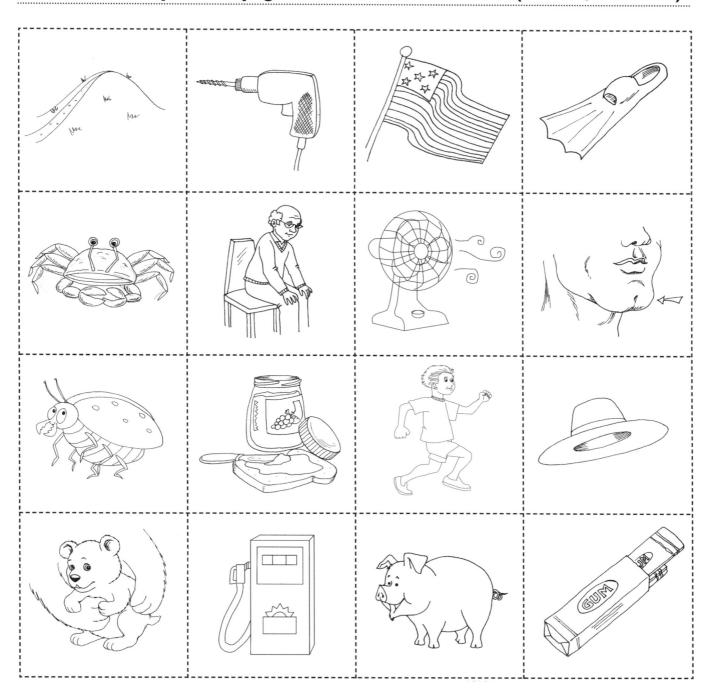

continued on next page

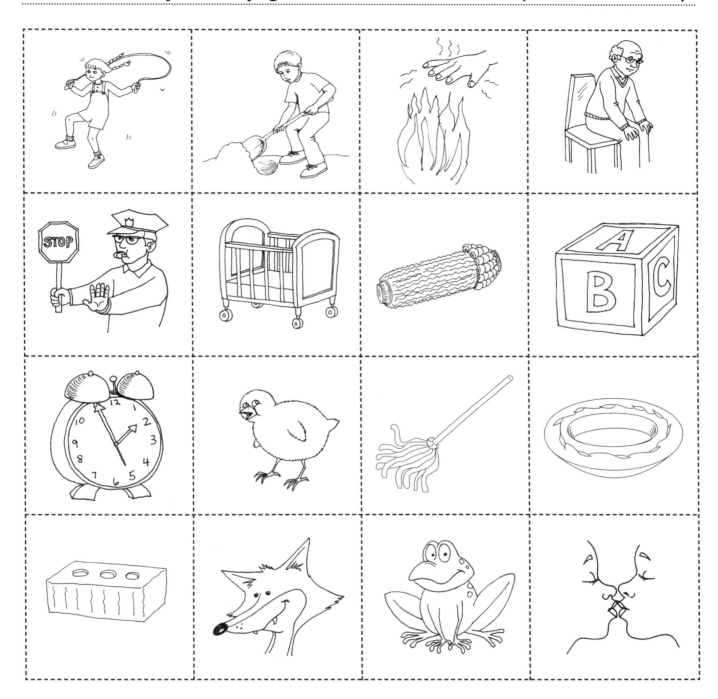

i fish   o dog   ODDS & ENDS

continued on next page

short vowels (inside i, o sounds)

continued on next page

short vowels (inside i, u sounds)

i fish   u bus   **ODDS & ENDS**

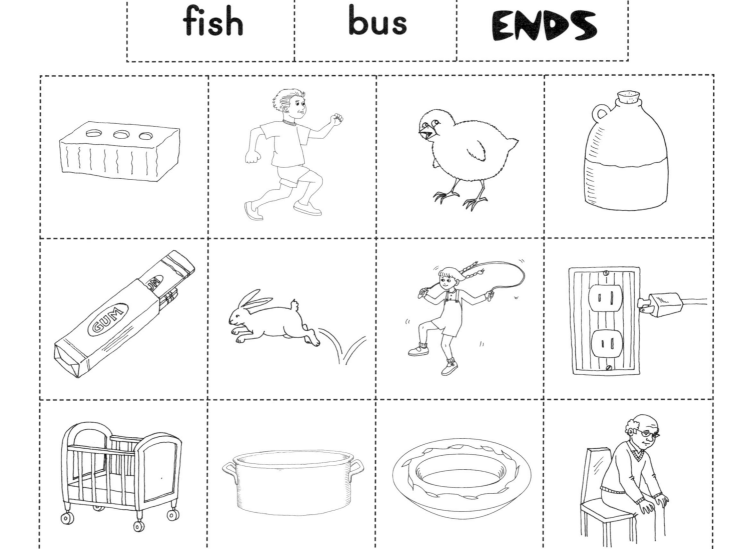

continued on next page

short vowels (inside i, u sounds)

o dog

a cat

continued on next page

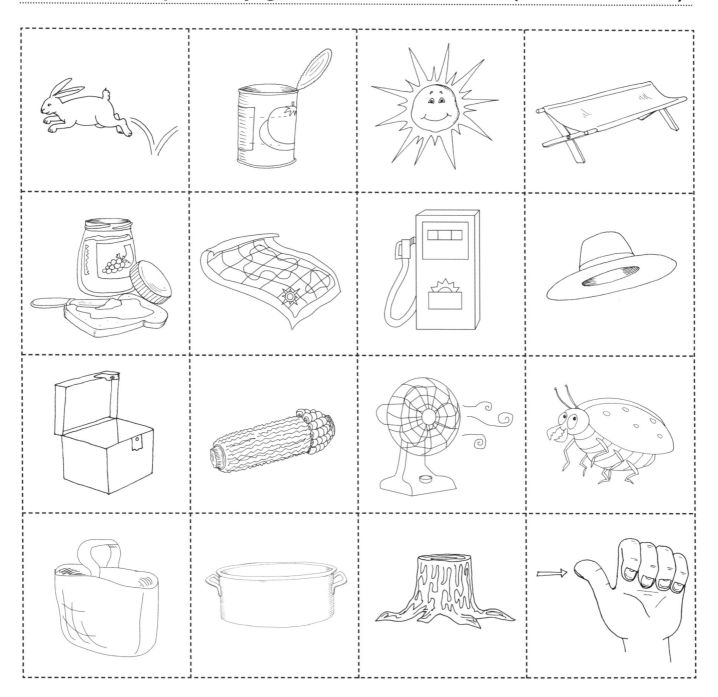

o ![dog] dog

e ![desk] desk

continued on next page

o dog

e desk

ODDS & ENDS

continued on next page

short vowels (inside o, e sounds)

continued on next page

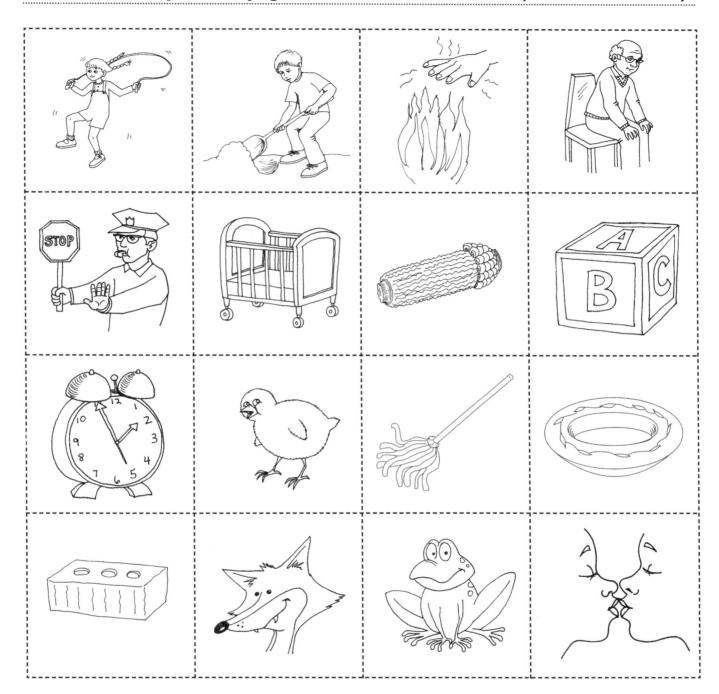

o dog   i fish   ODDS & ENDS

continued on next page

continued on next page

short vowels (inside o, u sounds)

| o 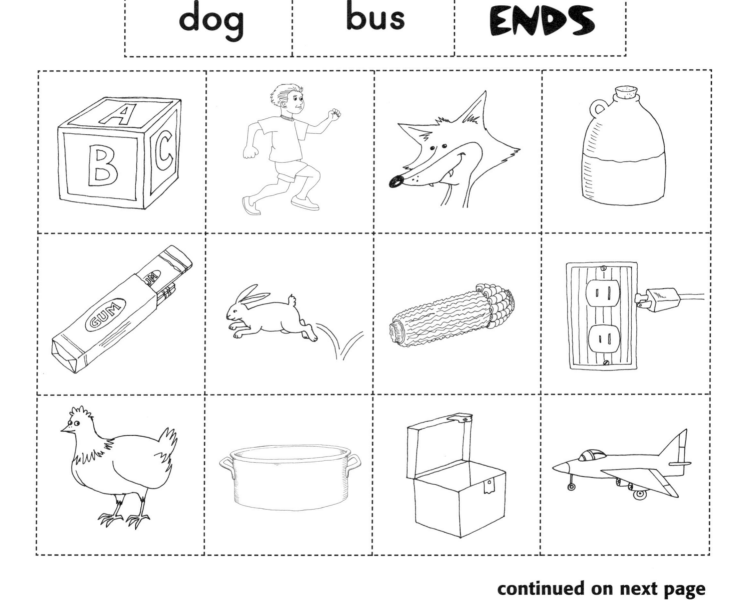 dog | u bus | ODDS & ENDS |

continued on next page

continued on next page

continued on next page

continued on next page

continued on next page

u — bus

a — cat

continued on next page

continued from previous page   **short vowels (inside u, a sounds)**

u 🚌 bus   a 🐱 cat   ODDS & ENDS

continued on next page

short vowels (inside u, a sounds)

continued on next page

short vowels (inside u, o sounds)

137

u   bus   o   dog   **ODDS & ENDS**

continued on next page

u bus   **i** fish

continued on next page

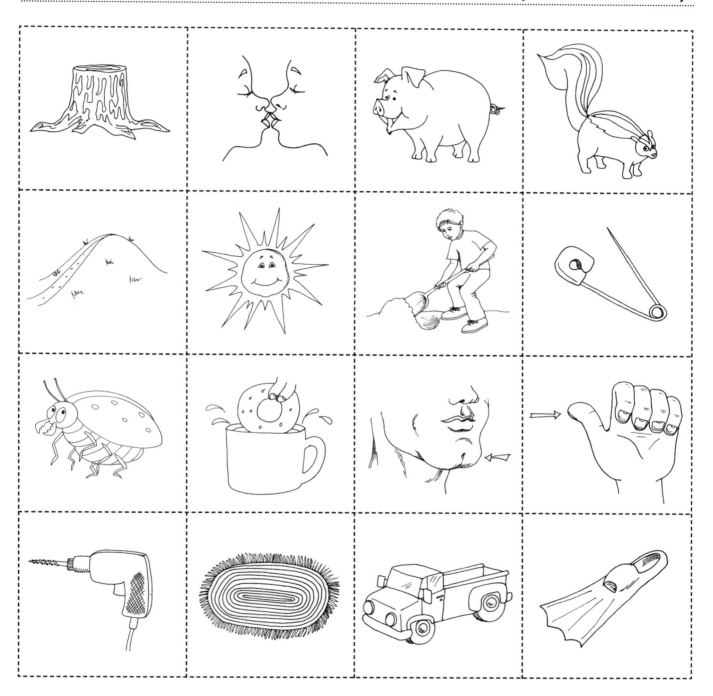

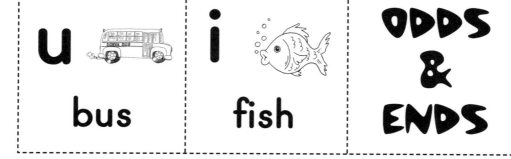

u — bus   i — fish   ODDS & ENDS

continued on next page

short vowels (inside u, i sounds)

continued on next page

u — bus   e — desk   ODDS & ENDS

continued on next page

Section V

Short to Long Vowel and Long to Long Vowel Comparison Sorts
Late Beginning Level/Early-Middle Transitional Level

Your students are ready to study the differences between long and short vowels when they begin experimenting with the spellings of the many vowel patterns of English. They "use but confuse" these patterns (Invernizzi, Abouzeid, & Gill, 1994). Students may be spelling the word *train,* t-r-a-n-e, t-r-a-i-n-e, or t-r-a-e-n, as they explore how to create the long vowel sound. At this stage students understand that sound alone does not indicate spelling.

To begin this study, students should compare what they know with the new information you're introducing. Therefore, I've organized this section in such a way that short and long vowel sounds can be compared and contrasted first. Once the students have effectively sorted these and noticed the differences in the sounds, they can do sorts comparing the long vowels for more extensive study.

A discussion of sort # 110, comparing long vowel sounds in the key cards *rake* and *bike,* might sound like this: "Let's see which column the picture *tape* might go in. *Tape, rake. Tape, bike.* What do you think, students? Yes, *tape* has the same long *a* sound that we hear in the word *rake.* Let's put *tape* in the long *a* column.

In addition, remember that a justified sort is a good sort. In sort #110, there is a picture of *mail.* A student may call this picture "letters." In this case, the student may express the need to create an *odds & ends* column for the *letters* picture. If the student can justify his/her decision, it is considered a good sort. If another student in the same group correctly identifies the picture as *mail* and places it in the long *a* column, then both students have what are considered good sorts.

Once students are effectively sorting the pictures by the sounds they hear, begin focusing on different spelling patterns. Eventually, you'll be able to move away from the pictures completely and sort only words. However, remember to return to the pictures each time you introduce a word sort for a new vowel sound. In this way, students will be carefully listening to the sounds in the words, noticing when a word has a short vowel sound and when a word has a long vowel sound. This is important in helping them begin to spell the vowel sounds correctly. It is particularly important in working with Second Language Learners.

a rake   **a** cat

continued on next page

rope   **dog**

continued on next page

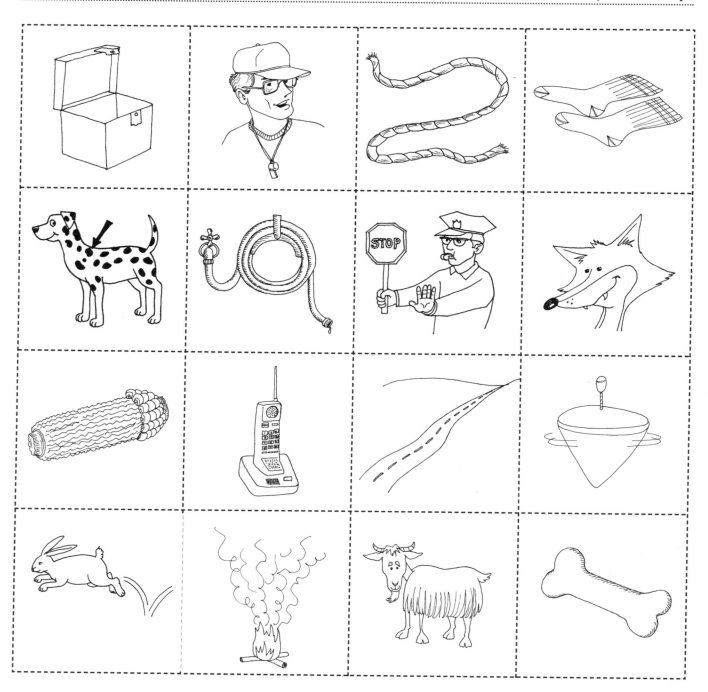

bike

fish

continued on next page

continued on next page

u [glue] glue   u [bus] bus

continued on next page

a   rake

o   rope

continued on next page

a 🧹 rake   i 🚲 bike

continued on next page

a — rake

i — bike

o — rope

continued on next page

| a rake | i bike | o rope | ODDS & ENDS |

continued on next page

long vowels (a, i and o sounds)

a rake

e sheep

continued on next page

long vowels (a and e sounds)

a rake   **e** sheep   **u** glue

continued on next page

continued from previous page   long vowels (a, e and u sounds)

| **a** rake | **e** sheep | **u** glue | ODDS & ENDS |

continued on next page

long vowels (a, e and u sounds)

continued on next page

long vowels (e and i sounds)

e   sheep

u   glue

continued on next page

long vowels (e and u sounds)

#120 beginning

long vowels (e, i and u sounds)

continued on next page

©2002 Teaching Resource Center

179

long vowels (e, i and u sounds)

continued on next page

continued on next page

long vowels (e and o sounds)

a [rake]   e [sheep]

continued on next page

long vowels (a and e sounds)

a — rake

e — sheep

o — rope

continued on next page

long vowels (a, e and o sounds)

a rake   **e** sheep   **o** rope   **ODDS & ENDS**

continued on next page

long vowels (a, e and o sounds)

continued on next page

long vowels (i and u sounds)

o rope

u glue

continued on next page

continued on next page

long vowels (i, o and u sounds)

| i — bike | o — rope | u — glue | **ODDS & ENDS** |

continued on next page

         197

Teaching Resource Center

P. O. Box 82777, San Diego, CA 92138-2777
1-800-833-3389
www.trcabc.com

Resources
available from Teaching Resource Center

Beginning Sound Card (item #53530350)
Beginning Sound Poster (item #53530370)
Beginning Sound Tent (item #53530360)
Beginning Blend/Digraph Sound Card (item #53530180)
Beginning Blend/Digraph Poster (item #53530190)
Beginning Sound Sort Cards (item #53530330)
Magnetic Beginning Sound Picture Tiles (item #53500100)
Short Vowel Sort Cards (item #53530240)
Long Vowel Pattern Sort Cards (item #53530260)
Literacy Task Cards (item #53590290)
All Sorts of Sorts by Sheron Brown (item #53520040)

References

Bear, D., & Barone, D. (1998). *Developing Literacy: An Integrated Approach to Assessment and Instruction.* Boston: Houghton Mifflin Company.

Bear, D., Invernizzi, M., Templeton, S., & Johnston, F. (2000). *Words Their Way: Word Study for Phonics, Vocabulary, and Spelling Instruction.* Upper Saddle River, N.J.: Prentice Hall.

Invernizzi, M. (1992). The Vowel and What Follows: A Phonological Frame of Orthographic Analysis, pp. 105-136 in *Development of Orthographic Knowledge and the Foundations of Literacy: A Memorial Festschrift for Edmund H. Henderson.* Edited by S. Templeton & D. Bear Hillsdale, NJ: Lawrence Erlbaum.

Invernizzi, M., Abouzeid, M., & Gill, T. (1994). *Using Students' Invented Spelling As a Guide for Spelling Instruction That Emphasizes Word Study.* Elementary School Journal, (95(2), pp. 155-167).

Vygotsky, L. S. (1978). *Mind in Society.* Cambridge, MA: Harvard University Press.

Index of Pictures

(horizontally by row from left to right)

Section I: Concept Sorts

#1   bike, boat, bus, horse
plane, sailboat, scooter, skateboard
sleigh, truck, train, unicycle
van, wagon, wheelchair, jeep

#2   alligator, rabbit, rat, tiger
bird, duck, eagle, ostrich
fish, frog, whale, octopus
kangaroo, snake, turtle, cat

#3   zebra, dinosaur, monkey, bus
ball, mice, swing, goat
boy, truck, book, ladder
bed, baby, skeleton, iquana

#4   blouse, scarf, skirt, belt
robe, coat, dress, shirt
socks, jeans, jacket, gloves
sweater, boots, raincoat, t-shirt

#5   cat, alligator, elephant, whale
horse, monkey, snake, rabbit
rat, turtle, tiger, zebra
gorilla, iguana, bear, dog

#6   zebra, chick, sheep, mouse
owl, rat, pig, penguin
skunk, duck, eagle, goat
swan, ostrich, mule, bird

#7   apple, carrot, banana, corn
grapes, cherry, pumpkin, peas
salad, peach, pear, fruit
lemon, asparagus, onion, lettuce

#8   bee, panda, butterfly, kangaroo
octopus, fly, grasshopper, snail
worm, spider, frog, ladybug
insect, toad, bird, chick

#9   fish, mouse, octopus, cow
lion, shrimp, bear, toad
whale, boy, seal, turtle
cat, frog, alligator, duck

#10   drill, skate, block, doll
puppet, nail, rake, crayon
rope, drum, twine, saw
top, tape, game, hammer

#11   eyes, feet, spine, brain
thumb, tooth, toe, hand
leg, nose, mouth, knee
chin, lip, ear, back

Section II: Initial Consonants

#12   man, mop, sailboat, saw
mouth, seal, mitten, soap
salad, mushroom, socks, mouse

#13   butterfly, mail, meat, boat
mice, boy, bike, mule
baby, bear, mitt, monkey

#14   monkey, braid, soap, banana
sailboat, meat, mouse, socks
book, saw, belt, mop

#15   bell, butterfly, bunny, ring
rat, robot, bear, rose
baby, rake, banana, bus

#16   radio, tiger, rain, tooth
turkey, tear, turtle, rope
rabbit, tube, robot, tent

#17   rake, ball, tank, ring
tie, boat, tire, rose
bee, rabbit, box, toe

#18   toad, peach, piano, popcorn
tire, tiger, pie, turkey
puppet, pin, tooth, turtle

#19   pony, pipe, needle, nurse
nose, pail, pear, nail
nest, pillow, necklace, penguin

#20   paint, nine, toe, peanut
name, tire, pumpkin, nickel
tent, pie, nose, tie

#21   nurse, gorilla, nail, gate
game, nest, girl, name
nine, goat, gum, necklace

#22   gorilla, fan, gift, toes
ghost, girl, fence, fire
five, fruit, fish, garden

#23   goat, fork, nose, fin
      nail, garden, gorilla, nurse
      feather, gate, nest, football

#24   dice, farm, doll, fox
      feather, door, fence, duck
      dish, dig, feet, fan

#25   dinosaur, deer, hand, heart
      helicopter, door, dice, horse
      desk, hive, dime, house

#26   duck, hill, fence, dish
      hook, fork, doll, hose
      fan, deer, hump, fox

#27   hook, couch, horse, computer
      cow, helicopter, comb, hammer
      horn, cat, carrot, hen

#28   cage, ladder, lamb, cake
      lion, cane, coat, ladybug
      cone, light, corn, lamp

#29   candy, horse, leaf, carrot
      cake, hose, horn, lake
      lip, heart, computer, lunch

#30   leaf, ladybug, worm, ladder
      lion, west, watch, lock
      window, log, watermelon, wink

#31   kangaroo, wall, king, wagon
      kitchen, kitten, kite, window
      key, water, wink, well

#32   watch, key, watermelon, ladybug
      kiss, worm, karate, leaf
      lip, ladder, window, kitchen

#33   kangaroo, jack-o'-lantern, kitchen, jack-in-the-box
      jaw, jeep, king, jump rope
      kite, karate, jacket, kiss

#34   jump, jam, vacuum, valentine
      vase, jug, jeans, vine
      jeep, violin, jack-in-the-box, visor

#35   jacket, volcano, jaw, kitten
      key, karate, jeep, kiss
      jack-o'-lantern, vest, visor, vase

#36   violin, yard, vine, yarn
      yell, vacuum, yolk, valentine
      yoke, volcano, yawn, vest

#37   yarn, zebra, zig zag, yell
      zip, yard, yawn, zoo
      yolk, Zero the Hero, yoke, zero

#38   yard, violin, zebra, yell
      yolk, yawn, zoo, zig zag
      vacuum, zip, valentine, vase

#39   quack, Zero the Hero, quail, zig zag
      quarter, question mark, zip, quill
      zebra, queen, quilt, zoo

Section III: Initial Blends and Digraphs

#40   back, block, bed, blindfold
      blouse, bag, bat, belt
      blue, book, bell, bug

#41   box, ball, brain, bag
      bread, brick, bell, bride
      bridge, bed, braid, bus

#42   braid, block, grain, blindfold
      blouse, bread, branch, bridge
      brick, blue, bride, blow

#43   sun, sled, soap, sleep
      sleigh, sandwich, sink, slide
      six, socks, slip, slippers

#44   snail, socks, sun, sandwich
      six, snake, snap, soap
      snow, sink, sneeze, snowman

#45   saw, swan, sandwich, sweater
      seal, salad, swim, socks
      swing, sun, switch, sweep

#46   spider, spill, salad, seal
      saw, spin, spot, sandwich
      sun, spoon, socks, splash

#47   scale, six, scarecrow, soap
      saw, scarf, scooter, sink
      seal, salad, school, scout

#48   seal, star, soap, stick
      stop, stump, sink, steam
      saw, stamp, salad, six

#49   skateboard, salad, skeleton, six
      skip, skirt, seal, soap
      skull, saw, skunk, sink

#50   shed, sandwich, socks, sheep
      shelf, shell, sun, ship
      shrimp, six, soap, sink

#51   cake, clap, claw, can
      cow, clock, comb, cleat
      cup, cloud, cat, clown

#52   crab, cash, carrot, crack
candy, crank, crash, cane
crate, crayon, cake, cage

#53   cow, cat, chain, chair
can, cheese, comb, cup
chick, cake, chimney, chop

#54   train, tie, trash, tag
truck, tail, tree, tent
trunk, ten, top, tray

#55   tent, turtle, twelve, top
tie, twenty, tweezers, tail
twins, twist, tag, ten

#56   thermometer, thirty, tent, top
tie, thorn, tag, throne
tail, ten, thumb, thermos

#57   frame, farm, frog, fan
feet, frown, fruit, fence
five, fish, fry, freckles

#58   fan, farm, flag, float
fly, fence, five, flute
feet, fish, flash, flower

#59   pig, plane, pin, plants
paint, plate, play, pan
panda, plug, peas, plow

#60   present, pump, peas, pumpkin
purse, price, pig, prune
pin, paint, panda, pray

#61   glasses, goat, gas, globe
gorilla, glass, game, gate
glove, gum, ghost, glue

#62   grapes, goat, grass, game
grasshopper, gas, gum, green
gate, grill, ghost, fish

Section IV: Short Vowels

#63   alligator, ostrich, apple, ox
olive, astronaut, otter, axe
ant, add, octopus, off

#64   umpire, axe, ad, up
apple, upside down, alligator, umbrella
underground, astronaut, Uncle Sam, ant

#65   upside down, olive, ostrich, up
otter, umpire, ox, off
umbrella, underground, octopus, Uncle Sam

#66   elephant, olive, egg, elf
ostrich, eleven, otter, off
eggplant, ox, octopus, elbow

#67   insect, itch, ill, ostrich
olive, ox, otter, inch
off, igloo, octopus, instruments

#68   elf, umpire, eleven, elephant
upside down, elbow, Uncle Sam, up
eggplant, umbrella, egg, underground

#69   ill, upside down, insect, umpire
up, itch, inch, underground
igloo, instruments, Uncle Sam, umbrella

#70   astronaut, add, itch, axe
insect, apple, ill, alligator
inch, ant, igloo, instruments

#71   up, add, astronaut, ant
upside down, alligator, underground, umpire
axe, umbrella, apple, Uncle Sam

#72   upside down, eleven, elf, up
Uncle Sam, elephant, egg, underground
umpire, elbow, umbrella, eggplant

#73   block, flag, mop, bus
bat, fox, frog, man
clock, crab, chop, doll
hop, can, bath, cot
jam, map, gas, hat
box, cob, fan, pan
bag, pot, hot, stop

#74   map, bat, doll, pot
cob, van, block, chick
fish, clock, man, bag
flag, lip, frog, cot
can, fan, dish, hat
mop, fox, gas, pan
jam, hop, box, chop

#75   dish, fan, brick, chin
flag, drill, hat, crib
fin, jam, hill, gas
chick, crab, pig, map
pan, pin, van, skip
man, bat, can, sit
dig, bath, kiss, bag

#76   van, fox, pan, pin
pig, man, chick, crab
bag, bat, box, can
fan, fin, hat, skip
sit, block, flag, drill
chin, gas, dish, jam
crib, brick, cob, hill

#77   hat, flag, truck, bath
thumb, sun, jam, stump
gas, rug, skunk, fan
bag, plug, can, bunk
map, pan, jug, cub
van, run, bat, gum
dunk, crab, bug, man

#78   plug, bag, chick, can
van, cub, bat, jug
dish, pan, run, gum
bug, man, jam, fish
hat, crab, stump, truck
flag, lip, thumb, sun
rug, fan, skunk, gas

#79   chin, bat, sit, hill
fin, bag, can, pan
man, map, drill, van
fan, chick, pin, crab
kiss, crib, jam, pig
brick, bath, gas, skip
flag, dish, dig, hat

#80   can, pan, chick, bat
jug, brick, van, crib
dish, pin, man, bag
hill, drill, flag, fin
crab, sit, fan, chin
bug, jam, run, hat
cub, gas, pig, gum

#81   hop, hill, chin, chop
fin, doll, cot, pig
box, drill, pot, pin
skip, dig, hot, sit
stop, crib, cob, block
clock, chick, mop, dish
brick, fox, frog, kiss

#82   block, cob, sit, bag
crib, can, mop, dish
chick, clock, brick, fox
hop, chin, chop, pig
drill, gas, box, crab
frog, doll, pin, pot
fin, hill, cot, fan

#83   dish, cub, sit, dunk
plug, crib, jug, skip
chick, gum, brick, run
bunk, dig, bug, chin
stump, pig, thumb, drill
skunk, hill, rug, fin
sun, pin, truck, kiss

#84   brick, run, chick, jug
gum, hop, skip, plug
crib, pot, dish, sit
stump, mop, pig, skunk
hill, sun, doll, pin
bug, chop, chin, thumb
drill, rug, truck, fin

#85   block, flag, mop, van
bat, fox, frog, man
clock, crab, chop, doll
hop, can, bath, cot
jam, map, gas, hat
box, cob, fan, pan
bag, pot, hot, stop

#86   block, flag, mop, van
truck, fox, frog, man
clock, crab, chop, doll
hop, can, sun, cot
jam, map, gas, hat
box, cob, fan, bug
bag, pot, stump, thumb

#87   hop, bell, bed, chop
fence, doll, cot, leg
box, dress, pot, men
neck, nest, hot, peg
stop, vest, cob, block
clock, jet, mop, hen
tent, fox, frog, ten

#88   hop, bell, bed, chop
fence, doll, thumb, leg
box, dress, pot, men
sun, nest, cot, stump
hen, vest, jet, block
clock, bug, mop, truck
tent, fox, frog, ten

#89   hop, hill, chin, chop
fin, doll, cot, pig
box, drill, pot, pin
skip, dig, hot, sit
stop, crib, cob, block
clock, chick, mop, dish
brick, fox, frog, kiss

#90   block, skip, sit, bag
crib, can, mop, dish
chick, clock, brick, fox
hop, chin, chop, pig
drill, gas, box, crab
frog, doll, pin, pot
fin, hill, cot, fan

#91   mop, cub, clock, dunk
        plug, fox, jug, hop
        box, gum, block, run
        bunk, cot, bug, chop
        stump, stop, thumb, cob
        skunk, frog, rug, hot
        sun, pot, truck, doll

#92   block, run, fox, jug
        gum, hop, cob, plug
        hen, pot, box, jet
        stump, mop, clock, skunk
        frog, sun, doll, bell
        bug, chop, bed, thumb
        cot, rug, truck, dress

#93   hop, bell, bed, chop
        fence, doll, cot, leg
        box, dress, pot, men
        neck, nest, hot, peg
        stop, vest, cob, block
        clock, jet, mop, hen
        tent, fox, frog, ten

#94   hop, bell, bed, chop
        fence, doll, thumb, leg
        box, dress, pot, men
        sun, nest, cot, stump
        hen, cob, jet, block
        clock, bug, mop, truck
        tent, fox, frog, ten

#95   vest, cub, neck, dunk
        plug, nest, jug, ten
        tent, gum, hen, run
        bunk, bed, bug, peg
        stump, bell, thumb, jet
        skunk, leg, rug, men
        sun, fence, truck, dress

#96   vest, cub, neck, doll
        plug, nest, jug, ten
        tent, box, block, run
        fox, bed, bug, hen
        stump, bell, thumb, frog
        skunk, leg, rug, men
        sun, fence, truck, dress

#97   hat, flag, truck, bath
        thumb, sun, jam, stump
        gas, rug, skunk, fan
        bag, plug, can, bunk
        map, pan, jug, cub
        van, run, bat, gum
        dunk, crab, bug, man

#98   hat, flag, truck, bath
        thumb, sun, jam, stump
        gas, rug, skunk, chick
        bag, plug, can, neck
        map, pan, jug, cub
        crib, run, fan, drill
        dish, crab, bug, man

#99   mop, cub, clock, dunk
        plug, fox, jug, hop
        box, gum, block, run
        bunk, cot, bug, chop
        stump, stop, thumb, cob
        skunk, frog, rug, hot
        sun, pot, truck, doll

#100   block, run, fox, jug
        gum, hop, cub, plug
        vest, pot, box, jet
        stump, mop, clock, skunk
        frog, sun, doll, bell
        bug, chop, bed, thumb
        cot, rug, truck, dress

#101   dish, cub, sit, gum
        plug, crib, jug, skip
        chick, bunk, brick, run
        stump, kiss, pig, skunk
        hill, sun, dig, pin
        bug, dunk, chin, thumb
        drill, rug, truck, fin

#102   brick, run, chick, jug
        flag, drill, skip, plug
        crib, bat, dish, sit
        stump, man, pig, skunk
        hill, sun, cub, pin
        bug, map, chin, thumb
        pan, rug, truck, fin

#103   vest, cub, neck, dunk
        plug, nest, jug, ten
        tent, gum, jet, run
        bunk, bed, bug, peg
        stump, bell, thumb, hen
        skunk, leg, rug, men
        sun, fence, truck, dress

#104   vest, cub, neck, doll
        plug, nest, jug, ten
        tent, mop, hop, run
        pot, bed, bug, jet
        stump, bell, thumb, chop
        skunk, gum, rug, men
        sun, fence, truck, dress

Section V: Short and Long Vowels

#105　bag, rain, map, mail
　　　skate, cash, hay, hat
　　　can, tray, sail, bath
　　　crab, scale, snail, frame
　　　fan, flag, tag, tape
　　　chain, jam, man, lake
　　　game, gas, ham, tail

#106　hot, comb, log, cone
　　　lock, globe, mop, coat
　　　doll, nose, boat, frog
　　　box, coach, rope, socks
　　　spot, hose, stop, fox
　　　cob, phone, road, top
　　　hop, smoke, goat, bone

#107　chick, slide, chin, smile
　　　spider, crib, tie, dish
　　　fin, tight, drill, pie
　　　hill, vine, hit, bride
　　　kick, lid, lip, dime
　　　fire, mitt, pig, five
　　　fly, hive, pin, kite

#108　bed, cheese, belt, key
　　　bell, feet, shed, street
　　　shelf, jeans, red, jeep
　　　sleep, men, neck, dress
　　　wheel, leg, green, teeth
　　　nest, beach, bee, bead
　　　beak, peg, yell, fence

#109　lunch, nut, cube, blue
　　　fruit, plug, rug, June
　　　mule, music, skunk, drum
　　　stump, prune, sun, suit
　　　gum, hug, jug, jump
　　　tube, thumb, truck, flute

#110　tape, hay, hose, mail
　　　rope, coach, rain, bone
　　　sail, tray, smoke, skate
　　　comb, snail, cone, coat
　　　scale, nose, goat, frame
　　　road, chain, boat, game
　　　lake, tail, globe, phone

#111　skate, sail, slide, hay
　　　pie, tie, mail, tight
　　　hive, rain, spider, tape
　　　bride, frame, five, scale
　　　vine, snail, game, smile
　　　fire, dime, chain, tail
　　　fly, lake, kite, tray

#112　slide, hose, skate, spider
　　　coach, pie, comb, cone
　　　globe, nose, rain, sail
　　　tray, bride, five, dime
　　　hay, snail, tie, boat
　　　chain, fire, tail, tight
　　　smile, game, coat, scale

#113　rain, slide, sail, sweater
　　　skate, nose, spider, coach
　　　comb, pie, swim, globe
　　　scale, swan, coat, tie
　　　smile, tray, spring, snail
　　　boat, twelve, tail, tight
　　　cone, dime, twins, vine

#114　mail, sail, cube, tape
　　　rain, blue, skate, fruit
　　　tray, hay, prune, flute
　　　lake, music, frame, snail
　　　mule, tube, scale, chain
　　　June, suit, game, tail

#115　tape, jeep, sail, cheese
　　　mail, feet, street, hay
　　　rain, tray, skate, key
　　　lake, sleep, tail, bee
　　　frame, wheel, bead, game
　　　scale, beak, beach, chain
　　　green, snail, teeth, jeans

#116　tape, feet, hay, cube
　　　mail, key, rain, street
　　　blue, sail, cheese, skate
　　　fruit, frame, jeans, music
　　　tube, prune, mule, bee
　　　sleep, wheel, beach, June
　　　snail, beak, suit, tail

#117　hat, truck, scale, cube
　　　mouth, key, rain, nickel
　　　blue, sail, cheese, skate
　　　fruit, tray, panda, music
　　　flute, bead, mule, bee
　　　king, wheel, beach, June
　　　snail, beak, helicopter, tail

#118　feet, slide, cheese, smile
　　　spider, key, tie, jeep
　　　jeans, tight, street, pie
　　　teeth, vine, beach, bride
　　　wheel, bee, beak, dime
　　　fire, bead, tree, five
　　　fly, hive, sleep, kite

#119   music, jeans, jeep, cheese
        fruit, street, cube, blue
        beak, key, feet, prune
        bee, June, teeth, suit
        flute, sleep, mule, beach
        bead, tree, wheel, tube

#120   tie, jeans, jeep, cheese
        fruit, tight, pie, blue
        tube, key, feet, prune
        cube, vine, June, mule
        bride, street, sleep, wheel
        suit, dime, music, kite
        five, fire, hive, green

#121   tie, jeans, jeep, cheese
        fruit, whisker, pie, blue
        tube, key, feet, x-ray
        cube, vine, June, mule
        bride, spring, splash, wheel
        shrimp, dime, tight, skateboard
        swing, fire, flute, green

#122   cheese, comb, street, cone
        jeans, globe, jeep, coat
        feet, nose, boat, key
        wheel, coach, rope, beak
        beach, hose, bee, sleep
        bead, phone, road, green
        teeth, smoke, goat, bone

#123   cheese, hay, street, mail
        jeans, skate, jeep, tray
        feet, rain, sail, key
        wheel, tape, scale, beak
        beach, tail, bee, sleep
        bead, frame, beach, green
        teeth, chain, snail, game

#124   rope, phone, street, mail
        jeans, skate, jeep, coach
        hose, rain, sail, key
        road, tape, scale, beak
        beach, coat, bee, sleep
        bead, frame, comb, nose
        teeth, chain, snail, boat

#125   rope, house, street, mail
        jeans, skate, blouse, coach
        hose, rain, sail, key
        road, tape, book, beak
        beach, coat, bee, sleep
        bead, frame, crown, nose
        clown, chain, snail, boat

#126   tie, flute, slide, smile
        fruit, tight, pie, blue
        tube, spider, fly, prune
        cube, vine, June, mule
        bride, five, fire, hive
        suit, dime, music, kite

#127   cone, flute, nose, globe
        fruit, boat, comb, blue
        tube, coat, bone, prune
        cube, smoke, June, mule
        coach, goat, rope, phone
        suit, road, music, hose

#128   cone, tie, nose, globe
        fruit, pie, comb, tight
        tube, fly, bone, prune
        cube, vine, June, mule
        dime, kite, bride, phone
        suit, road, music, hose
        fire, rope, five, hive

#129   cone, June, nose, globe
        heart, five, comb, tight
        tube, fly, hook, prune
        jaw, vine, mitt, mule
        dime, kite, bride, phone
        suit, road, music, hose
        lock, rope, jug, hive